AMPLEFORTH'S MISCELLANY

MICHAEL KARL RITCHIE

D1361818

Winter Goose
PUBLISHING
where words take flight

Winter Goose Publishing
45 Lafayette Road #114
North Hampton, NH 03862

www.wintergoosepublishing.com
Contact Information: info@wintergoosepublishing.com

Ampleforth's Miscellany

COPYRIGHT © 2017 by Michael Karl Ritchie

First Edition, February 2017

Cover Design by Winter Goose Publishing
Art by Sioux
Typesetting by Odyssey Publishing

ISBN: 978-1-941058-62-6

Published in the United States of America

"And a few cubicles away a mild, ineffectual, dreamy creature named Ampleforth, with very hairy ears and a surprising talent for juggling with rhymes and meters, was engaged in producing garbled versions—definitive texts, they were called—of poems which had become ideologically offensive but which for one reason or another were to be retained in the anthologies."

—George Orwell, *1984.*

Contents

A is for Atom

(2001) 30 Min. Color. An animated cartoon which graphically traces the discovery and development of atomic energy from the first atom smashing.

The Cincinnati skyline explodes:
the Carew tower shudders under pyro bursts
and then collapses, spewing glass debris.

A rolling ball of flame broils the winged pigs
in the Ohio River. Dangling from swings,
children have no place to duck and cover.

In Fountain Square, the upraised bronze arms
melt and pool in their porphyry base.
Union Central's a gutted conch shell.

As far away as the Busy Bee, soundwaves
crumple the walls, wad them up, and strafe
what used to be Virginia Bakery.

It cost a million just to shoot this scene:
wild puffs of ash matted against the blue,
then superimposed in the final translate.

How it looks is all that matters.
Pictograms eviscerate the language
here in the dark where we watch ourselves die,
where memory lasts only as long as acetate.

Au Hazard Balthazar

(1966) Following his own aesthetic to "make visible, what without you, might never have been seen," Robert Bresson focuses on faith through the story of Marie and her beloved donkey Balthazaar.

Scents and colors seem the same
year after year after the rain,
but nothing's ever really the same:
the new is renewed just in refrain.

The new is what it's all about:
apples and pears appear tears
across an arabesque Romaunt
where ardor shears apart in wars.

No longer among us, the lost
inhabit and dream the mind,
ghostwriting whatever the cost;
rebirth doesn't redeem its kind.

Blind to change, we seem the same
as those who came before the rain;
blindness helps us remain the same.
The new is renewed just in refrain.

There is always promise in truly new
images perched on stems that stretch out thought,
perfuming without knowing that they do
subtle variations on the standard plot.

The new rejoice in being so alive
that darkness pearls into white feathery
whiffs, wild dervishes whom bells revive
in crowds, each a unique identity.

Peeling back lips, botanists botch the task
of catching what evaporates in air,
listening for whispers behind the mask,
if ever anything was really there.

Big Day in Bogo

(1967) 15 Min. Good conquers evil in an African village in the Cameroons
that rids itself of the medicine, man's charms, and the dreaded malarial
mosquito with the help of DDT supplied by UNICEF.

A patron at the desk hums the melody he wants.
Some nuns bicker over who will get the slides
of birds and trees. A man in a sleazy raincoat
leaves you his hotel room number
and two shopping bags full of clothes.

The man who likes to have an argument comes in
and passes out Xerox copies of his college degree.
Local schizophrenics start singing at the turntables.

A follow-up on the supplement
to the seventh interdepartmental questionnaire
has just been sent down for everyone to fill out:
"No one is allowed to leave the building before nine o'clock,
but no one is allowed to be in the building after nine either."

The carrousel slide projector you're demonstrating
jams on a native breastfeeding her child,
and the Citizens for Decency storm out of the room.
Upstairs the projectionist has lost the loop
and King Kong is eaten up by white space
            before he can lay a finger on Fay Wray.

Former employees you thought were dead
            show up to listen to poetry records.
A patron at the desk starts screaming in your face
and you are going to have to stay as beautiful
as Saint Theresa.

The Blob

(1958) 86 Min. DeLuxe Color. Steve McQueen and his girl are pursued by a giant mucus membrane from outer space in this drive-in theater classic.

It pools and drools
beneath your feet
too cool to greet you
on the way out
of existential doubt.

Its choice is moist,
needling and wheedling
at the eyes, disguised
to make you sorry
for its hoary demise.

Spineless as brines,
it whines to be petted,
fetid as a swine
whose spine fretted
and regretted design.

Control cannot console
this droll spool of coal
that ignites depression,
and calls into question
what spikes the soul.

Burnet Woods

(1954) 10 Min. Color. A beautiful travelogue about this Cincinnati park, with its nature trails, artificial lake, and 1911 bandstand, here captured with a local polka band, as children romp about and parents bask in the autumn leaves.

In the dead of winter
driving me to junior high,
you roll down the windows
and quack at the ducks.

Who says being a housewife
Isn't a form of madness?
You roll down the windows
and quack at the ducks.

You do this every weekday
that my father will not drive,
and if the ducks aren't there
you quack for them anyway.

This park is out of way
if you're taking me to school,
but you stop the car and wait
to quack at the mamma duck.

"Look at the little ducks
all waddling behind her,"
and leaning out of the window
you invite me to quack along.

Because I hate all cars
and own none of my own,
I agree to join in, but
only if we sing off-key.

Circus

(1965) 105 Min. Reconstructed version of 1919 classic. The Little Tramp
draws a circle in the ring where circus acts once performed, and he sighs for a
lost love. Chaplin won a special Academy Award for this production.

The bedroom is not empty of objects
evoking her. I hiccup,
stand by the furniture and obfuscate.
For once no one will keep still.
I cease choking abnormally, frown,
and goose my mistress. She claims

that my love hasn't been satisfactory.
I stare down the wall at a lake
of fire. A canvas stretches underneath,
taut at the edges. I'm certain
my wife is still waiting for my

explanation. I don't turn around. Against me
the spotlight strikes and recoils. My body
shortens above the roof. Nothing else
sustains my heart. Now I can't hear
her endless recriminations, the drum roll, my life
collapsing like a card trick. My wife
elopes with my mistress; they leave
an empty bucket beneath me.

In my fall, perjured yet gullible, I crack
then alternate all colors of the rainbow.

Coffee Break

(1958) 14 Min. Research shows that the seven out of ten employees who take coffee breaks cost American industry a billion dollars annually. Presents the workers' and the company's points of view, and asks what can be done about abuses of this American institution.

When I hold the question mark upside down,
I discover a hook to go fishing with.

Fishing requires patience and the good will
to throw smarter catches back in the water.

Sometimes upside down turns the hook
into a cradle full of spring flowers.

A leafy trellis hangs out like a rat's tail
or clumps of spinach ready for soup.

It's amazing what happens every time
a question is turned upside down.

But never turn one inside out
or you might spill the Milky Way.

Daylight Savings Time

(1950) 9 Min. Color. Symbolic, impressionistic history of the discovery and measurement of time, from sun worshippers to underwater wrist watches,

If Japan adapted Daylight Savings Time,
their economy could make an additional billion.
Everybody would suddenly feel better.

Time would not have been lost,
nor would they have to run to catch up to the West
if Japan adapted Daylight Savings Time.

The hour it takes to walk home from work
would slow us down to enjoy the full sunset.
Everybody would suddenly feel better.

Altering clocks to keep science correct
could teach patience through origami
if Japan adapted Daylight Savings Time.

Who needs an extra hour on the Internet,
and isn't there an hour we'd like to forget?
Everybody would suddenly feel better.

Human time moves at the pace of moonlight
falling into its own image on a lake.
If Japan adapted Daylight Savings Time,
everybody would suddenly feel better.

Dr. Jekyll and Mr. Hyde

(1931) 85 Min. In this classic adaptation of Robert Louis Stevenson's work, Rouben Mamoulian elicits an outstanding performance from Frederic March in this print specifically edited for high school, with the infamous whipping scene removed.

1.

               Whoever controls the image

controls perception.   Servant and master,

         compliment each other,

knowing their place

               at opposite magnetic poles

        of society. This subjective

camera is supposed to implicate the audience.

         Then what a fright for women

to see their image   reflected in the mirror

         as a man. More surprising,

when Frederic March gazes into that mirror,

        there   beneath his black cape

        the director behind it all

is suddenly exposed.

        As the eminent Victorians knew,

a shadow government,

             unphotogenic,

               lurks beneath the veneer

       of civilization.

2.

Both director and actors have by now died

and become shadows   in the acetate copy

       of the explosive

nitrate original. The image jumps,

      bends at the top,

                                        refuses to stay framed,
wants to hypnotize its audience
into reverential   awe. There,
                in the dark, among masses
of unknowns,   the social
                propriety of colonial power
                                                validates itself
through the capacity to rescue from oblivion
its human symbols
                        of authority: the actors seen,
and the master hidden

                                                behind the

mirror.

3.
In this dub
                of a dub
of a dub, the gun
                        at the rear of the tube
sprays its surface phosphors
                                        horizontally,
reading from the magnetized heads
                        the little iron filings
                                        of light. There is a hum,
a glow, as two of like kind
repel,
                        whereas two opposite attract:
servant and master;
                                master and master-

                                                master.

4.
Through repeated copying, magnetism

                                                disintegrates

into a reverie

        as nostalgic as *Last Year At Marienbad.*

Voices

        become muffled; edges of bodies

                              fray

off

        into halide filings.

Yet the ritual

persists,

        as all around it bodies

shudder into atoms. Such is the process of re-

membering, the brain

              flattened out

onto a visual plane, synapses

        struggling to cohere, the same loop,

played over and over,

        searching for the missing link.

5.

Panting,

breathless, the image

        beneath the buried face

emerges

        framed as a binary opposite,

against which all who are civilized

              resist,

yet to which all are hypnotically, magnetically drawn.

Smile. That's Darwin in the mirror.

The Eclectic Stopsign

(1957) 15 Min. A tribute to Oscar Treadwell, whose midnight radio program mixed beatnik poems with be-bop, in this case Monk's "Mysterioso," while all the grown-ups were asleep upstairs.

Black keys, white keys, honey, where's the quarter tone?
Thank heavens for my radio, Thelonious Monk in the ozone.

Hearing Kenneth Koch poems on the radio, while parents
        bickered in bed,
I took solace undercover, with Thelonious Monk in the
        ozone.

Belittling and demeaning whatever at dinner I'd said,
my father made me an exile with Thelonoius Monk in the
        ozone.

A secret decoder ring must have been hiding inside his skull,
where else could that music have come from than a monk in
        the ozone.

He attacked the piano like Bartok, squaring the root of null,
cubing melody between a monk and his beloved ozone.

My grandfather preferred Fats Waller's scratchy 78 riffs
or his Cincinnati program that laughed us all into the ozone.

Beatniks in Mount Adams ran bookstores off the cliffs,
serving coffee, clicking fingers to Thelonious Monk in the
        ozone.

We needed jazz hipper than an accordion polka ball,
or German forever we'd mourn Thelonious Monk in the
        ozone.

Nobody was covering the outfield when Ko sent one over
        the wall,
so cheer poetry baseball and Thelonious Monk in the ozone.

Elegy

(1977) 38 Min. Color. Michael York recites Thomas Gray's "Elegy Written in a Country Churchyard," to scenes from St.Giles Parish Church at Stoke Poges in Buckinhamshire, England. Includes images inside and outside the church, especially the ancient gravestones.

When I write "father," I do not mean my
father, nor do I mean your father, nor
any mythic fatherhood. I simply
intend the word itself, so that I may write,
"Now father is dead," without meaning it.

Perhaps "is" itself has not content, so
that "we are" occurs at moments of un-
consciousness—though most likely we shall
be observed by someone. This "being
observed when least conscious" constitutes our
naturalness in another's myth of
us. No doubt what me most love about another
resides in those moments of her quiet,
meditative stillness, when she least suspects
she is being observed, least projects
her self-image as a wall. Therefore,
when I write "is," I do not mean my,
your, or all
Being, but rather the word itself, naturally
observed in its predicate.

In which case, what value has death
as a past participle? Does a coffin
house its coffin? The shell of an animal
echoes only the pulse of our ear. Thus
this past participle cradles no corpse.
In my vocabulary. It has no meaning beyond
what is provoked in response to it:
I intend it to shock, but not to signify.

With these things in mind, you may
finally see what I mean in choosing
to write, "Now father is dead,
the worm hooked to its screw, the ax stilled."

The Exiles

(1956) 15 Min. Using Czeslaw Milosz as an example, this short studies the effects of enforced exile upon significant artists from Eastern Europe during the Cold War.

They took away the color of your eyes and left me
this cubicle. What are eyes, anyway?
Color's so subjective, even white
walls gradually acquire texture.

Oleander never blooms here. Vodka
tastes flat as their coffee, and silence
has a meaning different from money
that changes color without notice.

Heaven is a walled-in garden. My fingers
point toward what array of names:
the bride's maze; the well-flower.
Only orchids could we both have agreed upon.

Behind shades, I watch the plane-tree
snow more numerous than bullets
things that do not register sound
or whose sound has changed to all but me.

Exiled from a land where words had power,
to a land where words drown words.

The Exploding Plastic Inevitable

(1966) 50 Min. At the Ludlow Garage, an underground parking garage where local bands like the Sacred Mushroom played rock music, Andy Warhol and members of his touring company, including the Velvet Underground, stage a happening, turning their video cameras on the Cincinnati hippies and freaks who attend.

This is not a face. It is the silence
of a face becoming pure face.

It is what I look out of, daily,
without being aware what I look like.

Except when reversed, as in a mirror,
rarely do I know what anybody else sees.

I am not even sure that I can recognize
myself when the film is projected before me.

All I see is the physical corpse that time
ravaged then discarded as so many fallen leaves.

If I had to see myself this way, repeatedly,
I would go mad, for this is not how I am in the mind.

This is not how I am when I dream, either,
and, disembodied, watch my body on film.

But film itself is an illusion, containing many gaps
between each image I can see when I blink.

So I have learned, when watching myself as a star,
the only real way to see me is to blink continuously.

Fantômas

(1913) 90 Min. Silent. Pearls are ripped from a royal princess, leaving
thumbprints of a dead corpse on her neck. Notorious as a creeping assassin in
black tights, Fantômas, a master of disguises, terrorizes the Paris underworld.
Police commissioner Inspector Juve and newspaper reporter Jérôme Fandor
set out to solve this baffling case of a corpse that keeps moving from place to
place for no logical reason.

01
The key was nipped by
an ostrich in the garden
whose dandelion
feathers were found in a trunk
with the groom's green tuxedo.

02
Cackling children swoop
naked from the asylum
whipping the bride's goat,
while orange snapdragons decompose
in the blue arboretum.

03
The bride's brain surgeon,
first with white, then red,
then tangerine wigs,
writhes among the arachnids
that feed on his intestines.

04
The bride is unveiled
and all the mirrors shatter;
her zoologist
reaches in the panther's cage,
to dust off the groom's head.

05
The first clue are high heels,
the second, a crown.
She cannot stand such

intimacy, blood
stained on the ostrich divan.

06
The bride's cousin hides
inside a living statue
hot to worship her.
The wounds of love are pearls
swallowed in fear and darkness.

07
The groom's parents search
architectural blueprints
to map the bride's flight
just after the zoo caught fire
and their son's body was found.

08
Police crack open
Cupid's statue to
find and dismantle
the skeleton of a child,
the heart of the green wedding.

09
The blues judge rules death
by electric guitar
snd rallies the mob
to loot what they want and hang
whoever gets in the way.

10
The old lady knows
before everyone else
who the killer is,
but as outsider cannot
marry and change the order.

11
The predatory
priest auctions off the groom's teeth
and rips from the bride

her pearls, veil, and fingernails
to sell as indulgences.

12
The bride and groom pose,
innocent before the fall,
on a ostrich farm
with a gypsy caravan
where panthers cage their lovers.

The Floating Library

(1967) A documentary on the Public Library's outreach to the Ohio River community, especially during the flood season.

When public libraries sailed out to sea,
books shivered their spines at watery graves;
animals were a faint memory
in bestiaries bound by briny staves.

And none aboard went two by two, but roared
a plenitude of conflicting tall tales
for the Cornucopian ear of God
who snored atop Braille pillows force-wind gales.

From salt to salt the crew evolved a pearl
that pooled its evanescent skein of stars
and leapt an oyster's tongue in onyx whorl
to dream from words the sounds that heal all scars.

For who knew where this raft of books would go
or which adults might find their inner child
within some scientific tract on snow
or some opulent Xanadu gone wild.

Frankenstein

(1931) 70 Min. The classic horror film, directed by James Whale, that set the standard for all gothic grotesques. Includes the deleted child murder scene.

Where did I get my monster? If you'd crawled
the trenches of the Somme, your comrades strewn
decaying in a no man's zone, or hung
on barbed wire, target practice for both sides
and made to twitch in rigor mortis smiles,
you'd know what creature God would resurrect
from graves. Or if you'd walked the London streets
and seen through fog disfigured shapes of men
without their legs—or men with faces sheared
of skin, a socket burn where once there was
an eye—you'd understand the nuts and bolts
of my contempt for science, mustard gas
and Gatling guns its finest achievement.

My favorite joke was making Karloff mute,
cutting the tongue from his Shakespearean
stature, compelling him to lurch crippled
by shoes that turned his need for human love
into a love that dared not speak its name.
The war taught all of us grotesques to laugh
at death and freed us from our social class,
our inhibitions. Sprawled on my lawn chair
in sunny Hollywood, I watch the boy
begin to trim suburban hedges, sad
that no one will produce my latest film,
a high camp romp about an aging queen
who's ostracized by all his former friends;
with garden shears he savages his eyes.
Oh well, the joke's on me. Perhaps with one
more drink, I'll take a final swim in my pool.

Franz Waxman

(1967) 20 Min. A memorial for the famous composer of such movies as *The Bride of Frankenstein* (1935), *Magnificent Obsession* (1935), *Captains Courageous* (1937), *Rebecca* (1940), *Dr. Jekyll and Mr. Hyde* (1941), and *Sunset Boulevard* (1950), among many others. Seen here rehearsing his oratorio with the Cincinnati Symphony Orchestra.

So banal in its normalcy,
so nondescript, nothing explains
this crematorium today,
where not a speck of ash remains.

Still, I have come to Terezín
as if these ovens housed small bones,
although no trace of children stains
one drop of blood upon these stones.

Instead I found some children's verses
and paintings made at Terezín.
Such scraps of song my choir rehearses,
so music may remember sin.

Some things should never be forgotten
to salve a new millennium—
where parents fight to make a buck
and children murder children.

Getting a Job Is a Job

(1957) 18 Min. The right and wrong approaches of applying for a job.
Includes information on self-analysis, preparation of data sheets, obtaining
references, investigating job opportunities, completing application forms, the
personal interview, and the follow-up.

I have lost both my hands.
I open an envelope and they fall out.
I put them back on and grope for my teeth.

Slowly I make myself up from scratch.
I am looking for employment. Please hire me!
I know how to follow instructions—

How else do you think I made it here?
My body has gotten out of hand—
it is inflating like a weather balloon.

Slowly I bounce across the gravel.
I would take a job at manual labor
if only I could get my feet on the ground.

Well now it is really too late.
I am floating away. I am decomposing in air.
I am becoming the snow drift outside your door.

The Gifted Ones

(1959) 22 Min. Shows differing opinions about the education of gifted children whose advanced mind distinguishes them from their age group. Two prominent educators discuss their views, and gifted children are observed in their regular school activities.

Is poetry alive—or dead? Or both?
What matters is that meter doesn't change
or garble nature's metaphysic growth.
Song, on the auction block, turns culture strange.

These losses are enormous on the stock
exchange, where brokers bet on futures, rue
the roulette spin whose snake eyes drop, and hock
what's left of pension plans to balance through.

Ignored and ignorant, the troubadours
seem threadbare hummingbirds unto themselves,
enraptured when some metaphor restores
feeling to sound, where dichotomy kills.

All that the poets have is wit to make
imaginary numbers calculate.

The Grammar God

(1957) 15 Min. Color. An animated film for elementary children presenting basic rules for formal grammar.

It belched. Semicolons lost their tails
and genealogies babbled on and on
without stopping to sip sweet tea
beneath an Arkansas summer sun.

It hiccupped. Apostrophes fell off their hooks
and swung skyward, dark wedges
honking in formation, elderly
fleeing the chill of naked trees.

It sneezed. Thick-headed and metallic,
its teeth grinding chalk across blackboards,
it spewed exclamation points as high
fever and flu exasperated its reason.

Who made the Grammar God?
Businessmen and conformists
cemented walls of rules around
the missing questions marks.

Home for Life

(1979) 25 Min. Adult. A sensitive documentary study of the experiences of two elderly people in their first month at a superior nursing home for the aged. Designed for professional audiences, in-service staff training, and all non-professionals interested in the problems of the aged.

And always we are being robbed of our
childhood, the house we love taken from us:
no alcove to harbor a last embrace
with grandchildren. The plants line up, dressed sharp
as clay pots to take lessons from the weeds.

And always we are being reminded
we shall never sit here again, absorbed
by histories a porch evokes: the lull
after a good meal when rivalries mend
and someone rises to help the others.

Not even naming compensates for the loss
of things which named us: adrift, the couch
swing with its three wishes; the bamboo
screens, rolled up and holding their breath of snail
ash; the unswept floor, blurred, insubstantial.

And always what we earn must be re-earned
in order to be kept. There is no lodge,
no stopping-off place for lovers to rest
their secret childhood together. This porch
we built to capture an echo of psalm

mourns us, dear husband, and grows transparent
as halos on the beaded lemonade.

The Immigrant

(1917) 20 Min. Silent. Charlie Chaplin stars as the Little Tramp in this troubling celebration of the American immigrant experience.

According to the label on these pears,
this tin has passed its expiration date
by more than days, apparently by years,
abandoned in the sand as surplus waste.

Pried open, inside wallow two dry humps
whose marrow of spoiled rations mocks and clocks
a taste for blood that borders on raw stumps
to turn a profit for prosthetic stocks.

Upon the label, missing children stare,
preserved without their parents over years,
trusting the state, completely unaware
of immigrants who harvested the pears.

Instruments of the Orchestra

(1965) 22 Min. A contemporary British composition serves as an example to demonstrate the various instruments in this British orchestra.

The mezzanine is full of ragweed
acknowledging you. You sneeze,
trip over your cello, and fall.
You try strumming normally, hack
and cough at the conductress. She asks

if the tempo is satisfactory.
You gawk through your glasses at her nose
of noses. Her nostrils flare overhead,
exhuming stagnant subtleties. You notice
the conductress is no longer waiting for

your answer. You hold your ground. Above you
some melody shrieks and wheezes. Your sneezing
echoes throughout the pavilion. Someone else
is arriving in the pavilion: you can sense
his hysterical screaming, his velocity, his nose
falling like a piano. The conductress suddenly
is flattened by a bellboy: they
splinter the pavilion to pieces.

After the inquest, atonal and entropic, you
confiscate, then catalog all of the noses.

Jumping Trains

(1936) 45 Min. WWI doughboys reminisce about surviving the Great
Depression through jobs from the Works Projects Administration. Includes
a tour through Union Central and a brief glimpse of the murals surrounding
the central kiosk, all of which have been torn down and replaced by a
shopping mall.

Resolute, two linemen cleared
the track that held the same longing
for both. On the worn planks
by the siding, copper nails all
shone with a fever forever brighter.

I drank up and stumbled by
with my signal lamp. Sandbags slumped
on the edge of my balance. Two switches
crackled in metal boxes on the pole.
Now she was coming toward us. Steam

slanted across her rinse of sparks
into crisp vapors glistening.
All up and down the line, signal lamps
flickered like disembodied eyes.
The icy cry of her boxcars passing

severed the fulcrum of balance and we jumped,
on either side of her, to be released,
settling on the lowest rung
like a postcard in her pocket.

The Kiss

(1963) 10 Min. One of the first "flickers," this lighthearted movie explores the Hollywood kiss.

The mall's a whale that swallows open space.
Dead authors stream across its vast crevasse
as crowds disperse and watch their quotes embrace,
chained nervously against a looking glass.

It's all an instillation now, for art
discarded feathers long ago, and flames
are only e-mails dissing cyberart
whose smiley faces hide the blush that shames.

Should power grids get zapped, computers sleep
and upgrade all their circuitries of health.
No matter what you do, consumers keep
expecting you to reinvent yourself.

Laika

(1956) A heartbreaking documentary from animal rights activists about the fate of a beloved stray dog aboard the Soviet spacecraft Sputnik 2.

1.
From hardworking dog-stars Rin-Tin-Tin
to Asta to Lassie to Uggie to dopers'
animated Goofy, Droopy, and Scooby-Doo,
lapidaries have memorialized their unconditional
love on the Hollywood Walk of Fame.

Outside a Moscow military research
facility, where Laika was strapped down
and experimented upon, the frisky dog,
cooked in space or crushed upon takeoff,
still poses photogenic atop Sputnik 2.

Rescued from an animal shelter,
Laika was a stray and, of course,
female, allowed, as a kind of reprieve,
to play with the researcher's children
before being taken away.

Although she can no longer lick
with affection any human face,
Romanian philatelists can still lick
the rare and collectable 1959
that honors her trip into space.

Back then, all over the world, from Gdansk
to Arkansas, little girls had rushed out
with first-aid kits, looking to the stars,
just in case that capsule might crash
down into their very own backyard.

2.
Rambunctious as a small pony,
you zigzagged, swiveled and swayed
to encourage me to run away
from all the bickering adults
that could only find fault with
whoever wanted to romp and play.

Aching to be hugged, I hugged you,
and buried my face in that wild russet
smell of gold fur, rife with
mulch from flowerbeds of irate
neighbors where you'd dug, dug, dug
to reveal what lay beneath the earth.

Those almond eyes wryly askance,
your Scottish ire provoked,
you balked at injustice or threats,
when all I really wanted to do
was climb on board and ride,
a small cowboy on a large dog.

Animals cannot help themselves:
they cannot stop behaving like animals.
In the living room sat grownups
politely discussing what to do about
you, now that my aunt was married
and ready to begin her own life.

Mathematical Peepshows

(2011) 10 Min. Short demonstrations of mathematical concepts:
measurement, topology, symmetry, and progressions.

A diamond pyramid
peaks, the instant light
triangulates the mirrors.

Its sharp horizons
slice as through a lime lifeline
of drizzle when torched.

*

What grow here are particles
that dream of being
faster than light to bend time.

Notice how the hair uncurls
peapods in a bean,
ready to droop off the tongue.

*

Between these crosshairs of light
multiples divide
droplets of silver and gold.

Each flicker trips the breaker
and flashes once, quick
signals with no trace behind.

*

Here a number of glass planes
angle for the sun
and focus mercurial warmth.

The fly has a thousand eyes,
nervous tics of doubt
from scattered perspectives.

*

Or can a sea-wave balance
on several tips
without having to choose one?

To break through this would require
contrapuntal worlds
from alternate paradigms.

*

Ecco-sketch a cloud, digits
mapping all the curves,
to capture refracting fog.

Each snap can trap what has passed
but cannot hold on.
The nub smolders wistfully.

*

A sphere should promise circles,
continuity of
families returning home.

What comforts doubt
swells, calmly bewildered
by the randomness of fireflies.

Mifune

(1977) 25 Min. A memorial to the great Japanese film actor, known especially for his roles in Akira Kurosawa's films. He became Japan's post-war generation's anti-hero, uncontrollable on the set.

Miserable from tuberculosis, he flung himself out
onto the landing and beneath the laundry.

Slugging his way across mud, he refused to die
until he caught and killed that bandit who hid among women.

Or wide-eyed with terror, he was a porcupine
quivering from arrows.

Or guiding a willful princess to safety,
his nobility was resolute and constant.

He knew how to die but he also knew
how to convince a whole town to kill for him.

The Emperor and he became symbiotic,
betrayed by the collapse of the samurai class.

Only once, they didn't connect,
and the medicine was slapped from his hand.

Mystère Picasso

(1955) 75 Min. Henri-Georges Clouzot reveals Picasso's artistic process of painting over and over and over and over again. What is Picasso trying to find?

I begin with a line
flung

                askew,
sensual,
      drawing that line
where it draws me
to risk
      making sense any
more than being gored
by a bull

        *

I slash without a care,
knocked

                off time,
unconscious,
      withdrawing that stare
where it singes me
to see,
      smashing sense no
more than being touched
by a sword

        *

I collage around a nude
laid

                              out cold,
flabby,
            spilling off the couch
where touch reminds me
to wallpaper
                        blue mosaics even
while being screened
from view

                    *

I stoop beside the canvas,
shocked
                              anew,
marveling,
            teasing that pulse
where it erases me
in dreams,
            smothering faults over
more by being born
again

                    *

I winnow out the excess
dredged
                        unhinged,
ruthless,
            ruffling the predictable
where it mimes me
to mimic,
            softening the punch more
often than being wounded
by words

*

I upend the consensus,
gleeful,

                      off kilter,
mischievous,

      staring down the stare
where it dares me
to dare,

      soiling oils more
so than being limited
by color

*

I rework the mask,
astigmatic,

                      primitive,
incestuous,

      breeding the hues
where they breed me
to thrive,

      cubing the form no
more than being transformed
to form

*

I level in the stars,
cunning,

                    witless,
curious,

      following the line

where it aligns me
to see,
        messing up more
often than being awakened
to awe

Naked Lunch

(1991) David Cronenberg turns William Burroughs 1959 novel and life into a metatextual adaptation, where typewriters become malevolent bugs that exterminator William Lee must control to compose the very story he is in.

Bored with your job? Come on over
and spend Saturday nights with me.

This old typewriter's aching to be touched
by your fingers. Never can tell what might come up!

These wounded bugs don't connect to the Internet,
but you'd be surprised how erotic that can be.

Staring into a blank screen, you're more likely
to find yourself total wish fulfillment.

All you need to bring is a six-pack of brew
and an overnight bag full of condoms.

I'll let you do all the kissing as we climb
inside the cage where centipedes molt.

Best keep your fingers on the keys, Kiki.
My typewriter's been known to bite back.

The Nautilus Crosses the Top of the World

(1958) 10 Min. Interviews with Admiral Hyman Rickover, father of the atomic submarine, and Commander William Anderson of the Nautilus, highlight a report of the epic voyage under the polar ice cap.

Somebody must have given him what
he wanted: an iceberg in crystal
icicles where light dipped
as slowly as thought crawling
toward blank halos. Planks groaned

against a razor grip that snapped nails
loose in bursts of brume, popping
with their ghastly echo. His ship stalled,
sails flaccid after losing their breath—
indeed there was no oxygen there

at the summit. Only white blindness
to peel like sunstroke from what little
remained of his face, concealed behind
dark goggles and whiskers of fur. Sight
froze. He could no longer tell where

one snow ended and another began.
This must be the rapture: cirrus clouds
made earth, where no man's boots left a trail
for those who followed. He had not thought
victory was oblivion, flags
planted for nations without borders.

Not

(1975) 15 Min. Linguistic study of popular American speech patterns, including the double negative and use of "ain't." Includes a brief episode where Donald Justice demonstrates the avant-garde technique of negative conversion, here applied to the "Blue Books" of Ludwig Wittgenstein.

1.
What is the lack of meaning
of a word? Let us not question
this answer by not asking

what is no explanation of the lack
of meaning of a word! What doesn't
the inexplicability of a word

not look like? Smoothly,
"Let us not ask what bewilderment
from lack of meaning is,

for whatever it is not
will be its meaning."

2.
If I do not give someone the request,
"Do not fetch me that red flower from that quicksand,"
how is he not to know what sort of flower
not to bring, as I have given him no word?

Now the question one might not suggest second
is that he did not go and look for a red flower
carrying a red image in his lack of mind,
and not comparing it with the lack of flowers
to see which one of them lacked the color of the image.

3.
I do not carry a chart confusing names and colored circles.
When I hear the request, "Fetch me not," etc.,
I do not draw my finger across the chart
from the word, "red," to the lack of circle,
and I do not go and look for a lack of flower
that lacks the same color as the circle.

This is the only way of finding,
and it's the usual way. We never go,
never look about us, never walk up to a flower
and pick it without comparing it to nothing.

Opera in the Zoo

(1962) 40 Min. A nostalgic reminiscence of Cincinnati Opera seasons that took place each summer in the Cincinnati Zoo.

If enraptured by the soprano, seals sang along.

It took one soprano quite a long time to die.
Just after you thought she'd gone, there she was again
in a desert outside New Orleans.

The seals sang along. They were having a field day.

The tenor bullfrog, a clodhopper,
stumbled and dropped the knife
in that final scene with Carmen.

And the seals sang along.

Poor Carmen! She had to lunge twice
before the tenor caught on.
She was so full of life, she could have strangled him.

Now all the animals upsurged.

Applause for the soprano. Applause for the seals.
Behind me, the woman whom I had insulted
in kindergarten, flirted with the Russian ambassador's son.

The Piano

(1990) 120 Min. Color. An exploration of the life and career of the great
American playwright, August Wilson, with special focus on his Pulitzer Prize
winning drama *The Piano Lesson* that addresses the issue of African-Americans
claiming their cultural heritage.

It's not just about the blues, although
blues is what everybody gets;
fooled by love and taken advantage of
is how you know you're alive and human.

A father doesn't have to love you
as long as he provides food, clothing, and shelter,
without skipping town to gamble on luck
in some junior league that will let him play ball.

And you don't have to love him either
no matter what the preacher may say,
'cause preachers need love so much
that they make themselves a God out of it.

A mother doesn't have to love her children
but she does, usually, and never forgets
or forgives their later betrayals,
because that's the piano she leaves in her will.

Some folks got it worse than others
because of the color of their skin
or the lack of money, but just being born
doesn't mean society has got to love you.

Pope Paul Visits America

(1965) 55 Min. Opens with the pilgrimage of Paul VI to the Holy Land and India, followed by his New York visit in October, 1965. Highlights include prayers at St. Patrick's Cathedral, peace messages at the U.N. meeting with President Johnson, Mass for peace at Yankee Stadium, and the visit to the Vatican Pavilion at the World's Fair.

The lobby is full of cellists
staring at me. I clear my throat,
walk to the desk and register.
Everyone begins speaking again.
I try breathing normally, smile,
and tip the bellboy. He asks

if the room is satisfactory.
I look out the window at a garden
of hedges. A plane circles overhead
dropping shredded paper. I wonder if
the bellboy is still waiting for

my answer. I turn around. Behind me
the moon rises and stares. My shadow
lengthens across the room. Something
else is in the room: I can hear its
heavy breathing, its hooves, its wings
flapping like a calliope. The bellboy
returns with the photographer; they
drag the thing from its corner.

When I rise, bloody but full, I bless
then autograph all of the pictures.

Porlock

(1944) 55 Min. A biography of the life of Samuel Taylor Coleridge, focusing on the composition of his "Kubla Khan," which was constantly interrupted by a county tax collector.

Outside my door
neighbors have gathered,

carrying torches
searching for a lost child

abducted from the playfield
by some stranger.

They insist that my writing
have a happy ending.

====================

Outside my door
nature collapses.

Ice cracks limbs of the old trees;
power lines glint in the frost.

Clouds darken and bruise
the punctured ozone.

Beauty becomes deadlier
to catch than any breath.

====================

Outside my door—
the unspeakable world!

Graduations and marriages
with a mariner on the moors,

an albatross of regret
hung round his neck,

afraid he'll be taken over
by strange social customs.

=====================

Outside my door—
The Lake District.

Sulking behind the lime tree.
I study my friends.

These are my credentials:
an ode on the slave trade,

biographies of the great dead—
Stop me if you've heard this before.

=====================

Inside my door,
a darkness heaves out.

Smoke stains the challises
in suspension of disbelief.

Ballads of colonial power
disturb the guilty.

Nobody wants my stock
of Oriental mysticism.

=====================

Outside my door
the empire collapses.

Reports of torture
are finally declassified.

The YouTube generation covets
more selfies with the stars

and military abuse.
All that's burning is the kindle.

====================

Outside my door—
fantasy writers

who want to be millionaires
or survive a failed state

mortgage toxic assets,
hijack an oil tanker,

New Millennialists
becoming lost boys.

====================

Outside my door
those who claim friendship

tell me to stop writing
and join them in the ice storm.

Only a select few, they say,
have the right to speak.

They do not believe
I am one of those.

====================

Outside my door
beggars rattle their cups.

State troopers and firemen become
telemarketers on the iPhone.

Ever since storks went south,
dogs have been scavenging the trash.

I'm putting on my rags,
to join the mob looting the stores.

The Pre-Raphaelites

(1983) 30 Min. A study of the major figures in the Pre-Raphaelite movement,
including Dante Gabriel Rosetti, William Morris, Holman Hunt, Sir John
Everett Millais, and Sir Edward Burne-Jones.

Fruit falls to the ground and its blood
swirls back up around me so that I am clothed
and bruised by your rejection.

I regret that the tendrilled sky
cloisters no arrow, that everything I see
comes filtered blue at the cuffs,

because that means you have abandoned me
among wastrel lilies and white rose

where once you retrieved the snow
moon of my eyes and, broken, smiled.

Quacks and Nostrums

(1958) 19 Min. Illustrates the error of taking quack medicines through the case of a woman who, after using an herb "cure all" for her attacks, is hospitalized because of a failure to get proper medical treatment. Work of the Food and Drug Administration and other agencies to protect the public.

When you hold onto something too long,
it turns to gold, then crumbles
like bone without marrow.

When you bear a grudge,
it turns into a hump
on your back.

Any words that you forbid
gain power in the silence,
then suddenly explode.

Just because you are a member
of the family of man
doesn't mean you are human.

Weeds thrive better
in the junkyard
of what people no longer need.

Still, be sly enough
to stay who you are
despite everybody else's advice.

Even today the leaves are greening
all on their own.

Questionnaires

(1966) 30 Min. A documentary about the Minnesota Multiphasic Personality Test and its applications to industry, the military, and schools. Demonstrates how emotionally disturbed people can be detected early for therapy and a cure.

Are you or have you ever become a stranger?
Are there more than one person who inhabit your body? How many?
What was their punishment? What was yours?
Were your hands bloodied? Did you feel any pain?
Did you crack apart on the shipping dock?
Where went your furniture? Your balm?
What are you still hiding? Why? Isn't it obvious we love you?
Is it in the bottom of the cupboard panel, the hidden one, the one you
        dreamed connected to the other bathroom in your grandmother's
        house?
How can anyone be specific?
Whom shall you turn to among all these broken pieces of your friends?
Who ever is whole any more?
Who broke the original promise that broke us all?
Whom else can we hang our guilt upon?
And who are you anyway?

Radar Men from the Moon

(1952) Fred Brannon: An exciting 12-part Saturday cliff-hanging serial
adventure where Commando Cody with his jetpack defends the earth. Fun
for all the kids.

And here we have film reflect its heritage
of carnival
            geek shows: helmet head
in a ballet of the fall,
                    where goodness
of technology redeems. Resurrection
          at mock speed
                 to overcome the gravity
of the situation, the serial survives
         by prolonging
                 climax. Already the binary
algorithms of UP/DOWN, ON/OFF, SLOW/FAST
        have been cubed
               on this buckle, with variant
indeterminacies in-between.
               How typically American,
        this dream
of a second chance,
        or of a third,
            or a fourth,
to thwart the threat of imminent failure
        by a faith
             in the transformative value
of science. But in fact we are witnessing the death
       of infinitude. For the recombinant
replication along each chromosome
          can only work out

a limited number
of mathematical possibilities. We now live in a finite
world, with finite
resources, over which binary
conflicts savage
the predatory
finitude of life. There is no immortality,
only replication. Nothing is reborn—
the four seasons are a cycle
vaporized
by the disappearing ozone layer
and the rising tides.
It is a failure of our perception
that we lay claim to the longevity
of trees, the spring of leaves—optical
illusions, for each leaf is new
and different,
made to fructify or perish
in the rock
quarry of our fall. That is why we watch
Commando Cody with bemused
smugness, indulging a childlike
wonder:
how to keep alive
a hope of escape,
how to keep the story going,
how to keep the story going.

The Redwoods

(1967) 25 Min. Color. The oldest and most majestic forests are being threatened with extinction. This film is an eloquent plea for their preservation and a poetic cry of citizen outrage against a growing apathy toward their natural resources and wildlife.

The answer is an arrow
The heart pinned to woe
The arrow in the scroll

In flight its feathers whistle
For leaves of vanished trees
The answer is an arrow

It hurtles from dark cursives
Whose riddles puzzle readers
The arrow in the scroll

Scholars are splitting atoms
Miniaturizing nannos
The answer is an arrow

Encrypted acrostics
Hieroglyphs on stone
The arrow in the scroll

It shatters consciousness
Each time it strikes home
The answer is an arrow
The arrow in the scroll

Senegalese Kings

(1999) 30 Min. A videotaped lecture by Professor Alex Darkwah, in which he proves that Ancient Egyptians were Africans. Tribal rites and rituals for the coronation of the new king and the ostracizing of the old king.

The instrument no longer plays.
The ram's horn he had put aside
shriveled in its goatskin balls
all reparations for slavery.

"The debts have not been paid."

Physicians for the African kings
transplanted a woman's heart
into an Africa no longer Africa,
but belonging to which clan?

Whoever has the most gold from the sun.

Not the whole earth nor the spinning globe,
but rather barbed wire around a tongue
that craps out on the stock exchange
one bar code for all body piercing.

Everyone has been tagged for the auction.

The slumbering giant has collective amnesia
when it comes to the slave or opium trade,
and none of its children can remember
whose skin has been flayed for their shoes.

"Maps name what armies have carved up."

A Sentimental Farewell

(2004) 35 Min. In Japanese and Chinese traditions, from the times of Basho
to Mao, men in old age retire to the mountains to reflect upon their life and
write poetry. Contains images from beautiful water-color scrolls, many of
which were destroyed during the Cultural Revolution.

It is not my voice I want in the poem,
but yours, reading my words and forgetting,
as only words can allow—my pleasure—
anything to leave you other than other.

How strange that this confluence of orange,
this brittle fingering of rags to vapor
awning over the afternoon prayer
could so startle, it would almost singe.

These words last just as long as your breath,
so I offer you red buds, black walnut, maple
for your voice to cradle back to life:
my testament, and place, and only children.

Shakespeare: Soul of an Age

(1967) 55 Min. Color. Key speeches from Shakespeare's chronicles, comedies, and tragedies are recited by Sir Michael Redgrave as the camera moves from landmark to landmark in Shakespeare's life and times.

Contrapuntally, throughout the house
clocks began to chime. Cats scattered
as time rolled in waves from the first
floor to the second, like ship's bells

driven mad by moonlight to dispute
the hour and the course of stars.
I paused beside a nineteenth-century
whaling ship, meticulously carved

using only original blueprints
and a piece of wood. No wonder
my professor of Shakespeare was going
blind. He lectured from his staunch

New England rocker on the folly
of trying to live a virtuous life.
Shakespeare, he claimed, knew
all the virtues were merely one face

of a coin that also contained its vice:
those who valued thrift would be seen
as tightwads; those who always told the truth
would be accused of tactless cruelty.

Not even the Puritans could have believed
from a state of fallen grace would come
American Edenic innocence, buried
chestnut in a rich pasture and nourished

by the blood (unacknowledged) of tribes
compromised out of the constitution.
Somehow Shakespeare had become the white
whale awaiting his riven blindness,

while we, children of the sixties, insisted
that the coin of the realm be purified by fire
and our lives be redeemed from the guilt
of unfair advantages. With the university

closed down by riots, Shakespearean paradox
could reside only in the privacy of a home
where each bell marked a different time
and innocence was the opposite of murder.

The Star Route Express

(1979) 55 Min. Vacation travelogue through wintry upstate New York; a road trip up rural backcountry, invoking the highway system of Dwight Eisenhower and joyous kicks of Jack Kerouac in disconsolate manic depression and Vietnam war-protesting post-traumatic stress disorder.

Bowling down the road in your '56 pickup,
I never wanted you to carry me.
All I wanted was a sense of community
to encircle like a parking ramp
that longs to reach its center.

You called me a stranger. I tell you:
welcome, we are of one mind now.
Breakdowns keep me hitching among
friends with whom I cannot live;
fade into vapor trails of departure

scars that friendship leaves behind.
Tollbooths line the highways
with debts I can never repay.
They are the debts of infinite longing,
the shattered face of a speedometer

waiting to be rescued at a gas station
closed for the night. You need a dead man
on your conscience before you can write.
The guilt of his death sets you free.
We are brothers. We tell each other lies.
We go riding to the wars.

Sundays in Church with Rosa

(1955) 24 Min. Research studies of Dr. Luigi Laurenti of home sales in
several cities reveal that property values do not decline when non-whites
move into the neighborhood. For community councils, service clubs, church
groups, intergroup agencies.

Here we may sit closer to God:
The pews are not reserved.
Everyone's an equal sinner.

To be a gentleman, shouldn't you
give your seat to a lady
so all may sit closer to God?

However poor, however unhappy,
no matter how white you think you are,
everyone's an equal sinner.

Hard on the back, hard on the legs,
work has made even kneeling hard,
but here we may sit closer to God.

Whether on a bus or on the road
or in Montgomery, Detroit, or the Capitol,
everyone's an equal sinner.

Sometimes you simply have to say
no more, no more of this,
in order for us all to sit closer to God
because everyone's an equal sinner.

Switzerland—Alpine Democracy

(1962) 17 Min. Color. An overview of this small, diverse, enterprising nation: geography, history, economics, and international position are portrayed.

Only the Swiss have holes.
Even their money is cheesy
with all those chocolate chalets.

They capitalized on
their mistake fermenting cheese.
Only the Swiss sell holes.

So many secret bank accounts,
no tax collector can figure them out
within all those chocolate chalets.

Snow made Swiss think of vanilla
icing around each doughnut:
only Swiss love holes.

You'd think they'd all be diabetic,
but they burn it off by skiing
down all those chocolate chalets.

Their mechanical clocks buzz and twitter
with cuckoos every hour.
Only the Swiss pop out of holes.

They teach us how to survive
playing both sides against the middle,
since only Swiss dig holes
through all those chocolate chalets.

Television Land

(c1971) 10 Min. Color and Black and White. A nostalgic and entertaining twenty-year review of the birth and progress of the television industry. This will be of special interest to media students and people concerned with the impact of this medium.

1.
Here they come.
They come forward
down a long corridor.
The corridor is filled with lights
so everything is clear.
They come forward
down a long corridor
filled with lights and reporters.
Now they slow down.
The one in handcuffs
is about to receive his bullets.
I watch them slow down.
Someone from the audience
starts shooting.

2.
Here they come again.
Quickly they snap forward
down a long corridor of lights.
Someone leaps forward
shooting. The one in handcuffs
looks surprised.

3.
I watch it again.
They come forward
down a long corridor.
Things slow down.
They begin to move frame by frame
through the stillness.
I can hardly bear to watch.
Someone from the audience
steps forward and shoots.

The one in handcuffs
   jerks back
   (freeze frame)
   and back
   (freeze frame)
   and back.
The corridor is filled with lights
so everything is clear.

4.
Again they come forward
down a long corridor of lights.
Again someone steps forward to shoot,
the one in handcuffs jerks back.
I can hardly bear to watch,
but I do watch.
I watch it again and again.
I start to cheer.

Underground Cinema

(1985) 30 Minutes. A documentary on the counter-culture and the rise of independent film, through Midnight Movies and cult festivals. Adult Content and Language.

Henry hoards his mail delivery
until a theater in heaven sunbursts
before a deformity of goiters that
entrances his head to pop off.

Vivisection of the child wounds
partridge wings beneath the radiator
where a scratchy Fats Waller '78
power surge blows the light out.

The brain's just another muscle
screwed to the end of a pencil
at the mercy of industrial waste,
brushed off as cosmic dust.

Virgil

(1963) 55 Min. At Walnut Hills High School, Rosemary Hope teaches a class about this yeoman who wrote a farming manual on the joys of goat-herding and animal husbandry, and who, commanded to write an epic honoring Caesar Augustus, tried but requested on his deathbed that the incomplete manuscript be burned. [High School Lesson Plans series]

Anaeas:
Anchises, dear father, I thought you were dead!
Climb on my back so I may carry you
from the fire devouring our city.
Without you, our family's history
would be blown in ashes out to sea,
and I, exiled among the homeless,
would have no way to tether the sails
of memory to identity and reach
shores we could call our own,
freely to worship, freely to strive,
and lie buried next to one another.

Dido:
All your words are propaganda
to justify the State of Rome,
so upon this burning pyre
of everything you gave me
I fling myself, childless,
cursing what you stand for.
Nations who cannot marry
bequeath to generations
brooding resentments
diplomacy will never solve.
Go bond with men of your tribe.

Volcano

(1960) 17½ Min. Hawaii's Moana Loa, Vesuvius, the destructive Krakatoa of the East Indies, and other famous volcanoes dramatically illustrate the causes, effects, and the terrible power of volcanic activity.

I love my lava lamp.
Its lozenges are dope.
Its colors morph and cramp
in sticky strands of smoke.

I love my lava lamp.
It glows throughout the night.
Kaleidoscopic damp
squids of ink ignite.

Now that the plasma amp
of my TV just blew,
without my lava lamp
I don't know what I'd do.

It draws mosquitoes near
and oranges with the moon.
Trapped within its sphere
molecules balloon.

I love my lava lamp.
It lets me dream awake
and watch blue demons stamp
into an angel cake.

Words

(1955) 30 Min. Interviews with famous writers reveal what initially prompted
them to begin writing.

Back from Church School, I found no one home,
the kitchen in disarray;
the high chair overturned, its wooden tray
splintered across the linoleum.

Our upstairs neighbor, who taught everyone
on the block remedial speech, had me stay
in, and gave me a book to play
with. I had to cut out and glue on

characters to make the story function.
By helping the author out this way,
I slowly realigned that wooden tray
and tried to find a place for everyone,

turning through the pages to discover
wherever was the word for my brother.

X Marks the Spot

(1963) 28 Min. Aimed at showing how cities have thrived when they exist
in harmony with their rural surroundings. Poses the problem of how we can
maintain or restore this balance in today's sprawling suburban regions.

What if you could not tell where safety lies
down Cincinnati streets after a rain,
its gas lamps blurred, lighthouses in disguise,
as girders pool into a satin stain?

What if your trust were suddenly betrayed,
by women, work, and God gone down the drain,
no roof over your head, a live grenade
now scrounging for a meal from the insane?

What if the comfort that you always thought
would ease your final days was false, not good?
A bill of sales that proved how you were bought
and sold before you even knew you would—
tossed into a common grave along
those riverbanks where you do not belong.

Youth and the Law

(1962) 36 Min. Pinpoints problems of youth in contemporary community life. Dramatizes the role of police as they work with community agencies to guide youthful energy into constructive channels and points out the unique aspect of juvenile law and teamwork with mental health resources. The role of "preventative patrol" is emphasized.

And don't forget those
who everyone says don't
deserve any help.

They, most of all, have
given up and can hardly
crawl out of their hole.

As the body fails,
light blurs around the edges,
catches fire, and burns.

Hard to see each day,
harder, each night, where distance
flattens into slate.

Remember how they
were before the accident.
They knew how to dance.

Zappa at Cincinnati

(1970) 85 Min. An unauthorized video of The Mothers of Invention concert, with Frank Zappa, at Music Hall in Cincinnati, Ohio. In the midst of a raucous number, Frank breaks a string on his guitar, but the band keeps playing as he restrings and retunes.

Where are the freaks of yesteryear,
Daddy Villon? Have they been strafed
by Agent Orange, paterfamilias
of the Military Industrial Complex?

No, they are hiding inside service jobs,
in service to God and country
as if that would put food on the table,
as consumers of an incurable cancer.

When The Mothers took over Music Hall,
a different kind of opera exploded,
a combination of Stravinsky and Varèse
ripped from the grizzled flesh of the blues.

The audience couldn't stay in their seats.
The aisles were filled with dancing
as Frank sarcastically insulted everyone,
ending the concert mocking "Happy Together."

The freaks, Daddy, have retired
to Assisted Living in Nursing Homes.
The freaks, Daddy, are the new zombies
feeding off the young to live forever.

Zero Sum Game

(1952) 15 Min. Color. Cincinnati as it is now raises the question of its
future. Realistic presentation of how the Master Plan focuses attention on the
problems of traffic, parking, housing, and slum clearance.

Queen-Anne's lace pearls at the border and hems
all Nature in, the scent of dark vanilla lifts
the veil, baroque curlicues quail, green stems
absorb the sun, as someone's shadow shifts.

Who was she there, tomatoes red, roses
instead of tulips, living in a dentist's house
according to rules lineage imposes,
pinned to a clothesline like a flapping blouse.

Who is to say who is one or another?
Wind shears, lightning streaks through the basement,
all duck for cover, hugging one another,
finding in comfort what family meant.

And just as fast, the memories subside
to find myself back on the other side.

Addenda

Some words are hollow reeds that play like flutes,
while some are weapons used to cause disputes.
Some words are cockle shells where sea nymphs dwell;
some, bones of dice dead poets toss from hell.

Some words are flashing neons hung from shops
while others taste like licorice cough drops.
Just crack them open for the thought inside;
their marrow makes a people be one tribe.

But death can knock the wind out of your sails,
twist love to a calligraphy of snails.
To doubt your words turns opposites the same,
but then some words become the things they name.

To live in words takes more than just technique:
you have to earn your grief and right to speak.

Most poems take their titles from real audio-visual films.

The following poems take their titles and film descriptions from *Film Catalog 1971* of the Films and Recordings Department of the Public Library of Cincinnati and Hamilton County: *Big Day in Bogo, Coffee Break, Getting a Job Is a Job, The Gifted Ones, Home for Life, Instruments of the Orchestra, The Losers, The Nautilus Crosses the Top of the World. Pope Paul Visits America, Quarks and Nostrums, The Redwoods, Switzerland—Alpine Democracy, Television Land, Volcano, X Marks the Spot, Youth and the Law,* and *Zero Sum Game.*

The following poems take their titles and partial film descriptions from *Film Catalog 1971* of the Films and Recordings Department of the Public Library of Cincinnati and Hamilton County: *A is for Atom, Daylight Savings Time, Shakespeare: Soul of an Age,* and *Sundays in Church with Rosa.* Other film titles and descriptors may not really exist.

"The Exiles" was published in 2009 in the online journal *Other Rooms* and reprinted along with "Instruments of the Orchestra" in the anthology *OR Panthology—Ocellus Reseau,* in 2014. "Fantômas" was published in the 2012 issue of *The Mississippi Review.* "The Immigrant" was originally published as "Extended Tour of Duty" in *The Gihon River Review* [Fall 2010]. "The Piano" was originally published as "In Memoriam August Wilson (1945-2005)" in *The Dirty Napkin.* "Quarks and Nostrums" was originally published as "Voodoo and You" in the Fall 2005 issue of *Margie: The American Journal of Poetry.*

"Television Land" was originally published in a small-press edition *For Those in the Know,* Meadow Press, 1976. "Getting a Job Is a Job" was originally published in different form in a small-press edition *Night Blindness,* La Huerta Press, 1976. "Elegy," "Home for Life," and "The Pre-Raphaelites" were originally published in a small-press edition *Closing Down the Hearth,* O-2 Press, 1983.

About the Author

A polyphony of tones better serves a democracy, as does a diversity of styles. Michael Karl Ritchie's is only one cornucopia, aching for a readership of non-poets. At the end of Michael's life, he has returned to being a defrocked librarian, misremembering the media department of the downtown Public Library of Cincinnati, Ohio, and rewriting their film collection, real and imaginary. In his retirement, he has boarded a blog called THE SPACESHIP, where his poems about real films are posted for free.

CPSIA information can be obtained
at www.ICGtesting.com
Printed in the USA
LVOW11s0338080517
533667LV00001B/80/P